Times Tables Fun with Naughty Katie

Lorraine Reed

Matador
9 Priory Business Park,
Wistow Road, Kibworth Beauchamp,
Leicestershire. LE8 0RX
Tel: (+44) 116 279 2299
Fax: (+44) 116 279 2277
Email: books@troubador.co.uk
Web: www.troubador.co.uk/matador

ISBN 978 1785891 670

British Library Cataloguing in Publication Data.
A catalogue record for this book is available from the British Library.

Printed and bound by CPI Group (UK) Ltd, Croydon, CR0 4YY
Typeset in 11pt Century Gothic by Troubador Publishing Ltd, Leicester, UK

Matador is an imprint of Troubador Publishing Ltd

This book is dedicated to my darling husband Darren who has been my soulmate since I was sixteen years old. I also dedicate this book to our three beautiful, intelligent daughters Jade, Rebecca and Hayley whom I am very proud of.

I would also like to dedicate my book to:
Haydn, Stephanie, Dannielle and Dannielle's handsome baby boy Oscar.

My dad (Dr Graham Clingbine) and thank him for all his help in getting this book published.

My lovely sister Gemma Sara.

My dear cousins Sharon, Richard and their two gorgeous children Jessica and Nathan.

My dear cousin Daniel.

My mum and Harold, my two lovely sisters Janice, Lisa and Lisa's beautiful daughter Elisha.

My gorgeous lifelong friend Jo and her lovely husband Karl and their families.

My dear friend Vicki, her lovely husband Steve and their two gorgeous children, Jessica and Quinn.

All my family and friends.

Contents Page

About the Author

Lorraine Reed is a mother currently raising her three much loved daughters Jade, Rebecca and Hayley. Lorraine taught Hayley her times tables using the method in this book when Hayley was eight years old. Lorraine has been married to her husband Darren for many happy years. She has always shared her strong views on obtaining a good education to her own children and hopes that this book will encourage others to want to learn too.

Foreword

I became inspired to write the book Times Tables Fun With Naughty Katie while I was attending a 'meet the teachers morning' at my daughter Hayley's primary school when Hayley was about to move into year three of the junior school. The teacher was emphasising the importance of knowing the times tables to all the parents! I was a little concerned about the way in which I would go about teaching Hayley her times tables at home as I had tried quite a few times without success. Hayley would get bored and show no interest in learning them. Hayley is the type of child who enjoys expressing herself through language rather than numbers and also has a vivid imagination.

I wanted to find a way of combining Hayley's interest in words and imagination together with numbers to provide a more stimulating learning experience for her. To my pleasure and relief, Hayley loved learning her times tables using this method and began to learn them very quickly and correctly. I also tried this method on a few of my adult friends who hadn't practiced their times tables since they were at school and had forgotten them. I got the same results from my friends who were very pleased with themselves. This built up their confidence in using mathematics. My friends asked me if they could also use this method of learning times tables with their own children. This led me to decide to turn my learning idea into a book not just for Hayley but for anyone and everyone who would find this learning method useful.

Introduction

My aim for this book Times Tables Fun With Naughty Katie is for the child to enjoy a fun, unique and creative learning experience. Please read on to ensure you get the most out of this book with the best possible results!

An adult should read one story line at a time out loud for the child to listen to, followed by the times table below it. Start from one times one and proceed in numerical order. Then gradually work your way through the book eventually reaching the end of the twelve times table.

Once you have read aloud to the child the story line which you are on, read aloud the times table beneath it in the manner in which it is written (not including the answer), for example "Because 1 x 1 is." (Pause for the child to give you the answer!) Remind the child that the end of the sentence will rhyme with the answer that they need. This should help the child to gain the confidence that they will need in getting the answer right. It is important to also remind the child that when they are multiplying numbers their value increases. Putting it in simpler terms, the number in the next answer will always be higher than the last!

It's also important to remind the child that every time they give you an answer, they must keep this number in their mind in order to have an idea of what the next number might be as it increases in value! Another great tip for you is to tell the child that whenever they are multiplying a number by 10 that they only need to add a 0 to it to get the right answer, for example: (2 x 10 is 20) (3 x 10 is 30) (4 x 10 is 40) etc.

Lastly, it is very important to make sure that the child is enjoying this whole experience to ensure that they are learning their times tables without even realising it!

One
Times
Table

The one times table explained with Katie and her little sister Misty

Come and learn your times tables
in a way that's really fun!

Because 1 x 1 is 1

Katie and Misty would like to share
their stories with you.

Because 2 x 1 is 2

Throughout this book as you shall see.

Because 3 x 1 is 3

The girls will teach you so much more!

Because 4 x 1 is 4

We need times tables in our lives.

Because 5 x 1 is 5

With enjoyable adventures thrown into the mix.

Because 6 x 1 is 6

The girls will take you on adventures to
Kent and Devon.

Because 7 x 1 is 7

Keep the last number that you said in mind
and you will be great!

Because 8 x 1 is 8

And remember the numbers get higher
and you will be fine!

Because 9 x 1 is 9

Whenever you times a number by ten
just add a zero again.

Because 10 x 1 is 10

I hope that this new style of learning
feels like heaven!

Because 11 x 1 is 11

When you've learnt your times tables,
be very proud of yourself!

Because 12 x 1 is 12

Two
Times
Table

The two times table with naughty Katie up to mischief

Katie felt poorly, with the flu.

Because 1 x 2 is 2

She threw dirty tissues on the floor.

Because 2 x 2 is 4

Staring at the clock and listening to the ticks.

Because 3 x 2 is 6

Katie knew it was getting late.

Because 4 x 2 is 8

She sneezed and coughed then sneezed again.

Because 5 x 2 is 10

Poor Katie did not feel at all well!

Because 6 x 2 is 12

But naughty Katie was still pure mean!

Because 7 x 2 is 14

So in a draw she found some thick cream.

Because 8 x 2 is 16

Katie was bored, which she was hating!

Because 9 x 2 is 18

Then while crawling around on bent knee.

Because 10 x 2 is 20

She smeared cream over every room she went into.

Because 11 x 2 is 22

Her mother screamed at what she saw!

Because 12 x 2 is 24

Three
Times
Table

The three times table with naughty Katie up to tricks

The girls went to the seaside to paddle in the sea.

Because 1 x 3 is 3

They splashed each other with jumps and kicks.

Because 2 x 3 is 6

Then a dirty trick entered Katie's mind!

Because 3 x 3 is 9

She pretended that she was drowning
and couldn't save herself.

Because 4 x 3 is 12

She thrashed around, creating waves
which were bouncing and shifting.

Because 5 x 3 is 15

A passing boat noticed the panicked scene
that Katie was creating.

Because 6 x 3 is 18

The captain couldn't shoot a flare because he had an empty gun.

Because 7 x 3 is 21

So he jumped into the sea and pulled Katie up to the Kent seashore.

Because 8 x 3 is 24

This was not the day trip the captain had planned on a peaceful Kent sea heaven.

Because 9 x 3 is 27

He pulled Katie to safety in his smart new suit now soaking, sandy and dirty.

Because 10 x 3 is 30

Mum could see the captain crawling up the sand on dirty knees.

Because 11 x 3 is 33

She apologised to the captain for Katie's naughty, dirty tricks.

Because 12 x 3 is 36

Four
Times
Table

The four times table with naughty Katie and the neighbour's cat

Katie caught the neighbour's cat
and carried it through the door.

Because 1 x 4 is 4

She gave it some thick cream on a plate.

Because 2 x 4 is 8

Katie gave it some tuna as well.

Because 3 x 4 is 12

Then she gave the cat more thick cream.

Because 4 x 4 is 16

The cat licked the plate till it was empty.

Because 5 x 4 is 20

Food was now covering what had been a
clean and empty floor.

Because 6 x 4 is 24

Katie thought he must need a bath now that he had an empty plate.

Because 7 x 4 is 28

So she put the cat in the sink 'cos it was smelly and dirty too.

Because 8 x 4 is 32

The filthy cat covered the walls with mucky paws and dirty licks.

Because 9 x 4 is 36

Katie knew mum would be cross with her because she had been naughty!

Because 10 x 4 is 40

Mum had to take a double glance at what she thought she saw.

Because 11 x 4 is 44

Oh what a very naughty Kate.

Because 12 x 4 is 48

Five
Times
Table

The five times
table with naughty Katie
and the beehive

Katie found a dirty beehive.

Because 1 x 5 is 5

She poked the beehive with a pen.

Because 2 x 5 is 10

Slowly and carefully the beehive began lifting.

Because 3 x 5 is 15

But how was it moving so very gently?

Because 4 x 5 is 20

Suddenly Katie realised that mum
was lifting the beehive.

Because 5 x 5 is 25

Her mother looked nervous and dirty.

Because 6 x 5 is 30

Mum was covered in muck,
from the dirty hive.

Because 7 x 5 is 35

Then suddenly Katie did something very
naughty!

Because 8 x 5 is 40

While shouting out "you naughty hive."

Because 9 x 5 is 45

And looking rather shifty.

Because 10 x 5 is 50

With all her strength she kicked the beehive.

Because 11 x 5 is 55

Some bees flew out and stung poor Misty.

Because 12 x 5 is 60

Six
Times
Table

The six times table
with naughty jealous Katie

Katie wouldn't share her wooden sticks.

Because 1 x 6 is 6

So Misty looked for some herself.

Because 2 x 6 is 12

But Katie wasn't waiting!

Because 3 x 6 is 18

For Misty to find plenty more.

Because 4 x 6 is 24

So Katie told Misty her sticks were dirty.

Because 5 x 6 is 30

So Misty washed her dirty sticks.

Because 6 x 6 is 36

Katie looked at Misty's sticks, all washed and
sorted through!

Because 7 x 6 is 42

She was a jealous naughty Kate!

Because 8 x 6 is 48

So instead of giving Misty more.

Because 9 x 6 is 54

She snatched all the clean sticks away from Misty.

Because 10 x 6 is 60

Then she ran away with Misty's sticks.

Because 11 x 6 is 66

And hid then in an empty shoe.

Because 12 x 6 is 72

Seven
Times
Table

The seven times table with naughty Katie on holiday

Mum took Katie and Misty on a camping holiday to Devon.

Because 1 x 7 is 7

Once they had finished unpacking and sorting.

Because 2 x 7 is 14

Misty asked mum. "Will the tent be fun?"

Because 3 x 7 is 21

Then Katie asked mum "will the tent be great?"

Because 4 x 7 is 28

Mum smiled while holding a rod, worms, some tweezers and a dirty knife.

Because 5 x 7 is 35

Then mum said "we're going to catch fish for lunch the way my mum once taught me to."

Because 6 x 7 is 42

So they cast out the rod with a short neat line.

Because 7 x 7 is 49

Floating on the water were some drifting sticks.

Because 8 x 7 is 56

Katie said she caught a fish but she would
not let Misty see!

Because 9 x 7 is 63

But all Katie really caught were the sticks
floating on the Devon sea!

Because 10 x 7 is 70

The sun shone so brightly, it felt like Devon sea
heaven.

Because 11 x 7 is 77

Then they all ate fresh fish on
Devon's great seashore.

Because 12 x 7 is 84

Eight
Times
Table

The eight times table with naughty Katie baking cakes

"I'm baking cakes today" said Kate.

Because 1 x 8 is 8

"I've got a plastic spoon for mixing."

Because 2 x 8 is 16

Katie spilt some dough but
there was plenty more.

Because 3 x 8 is 24

The table was a mess and dirty too.

Because 4 x 8 is 32

Katie loved the mess 'cos
she was naughty!

Because 5 x 8 is 40

What a very naughty Kate!

Because 6 x 8 is 48

Then Katie spilt all of Misty's mix.

Because 7 x 8 is 56

Poor Misty had to then mix more.

Because 8 x 8 is 64

Eventually the cakes looked pretty
and smelt heavenly too.

Because 9 x 8 is 72

Finally, Misty could enjoy her
yummy cakes and lovely tea.

Because 10 x 8 is 80

But then in came naughty Katie Kate.

Because 11 x 8 is 88

She smashed poor Misty's cakes
with mighty kicks!

Because 12 x 8 is 96

Nine
Times
Table

The nine times table with Katie late for school again

Mum tried to teach Katie how to tell the time.

Because 1 x 9 is 9

So Katie would be ready early for school
and stop keeping her waiting!

Because 2 x 9 is 18

Katie being ready on time sounded like a
morning spent in heaven.

Because 3 x 9 is 27

Washed, ready and out the door
without Katie's usual dirty tricks.

Because 4 x 9 is 36

But Katie quite enjoyed her lazy, naughty life.

Because 5 x 9 is 45

So Katie still had to be pulled out of bed
shouting "lift me more!"

Because 6 x 9 is 54

Then Katie stood in front of the mirror and she wouldn't let Misty see.

Because 7 x 9 is 63

Peaceful mornings for mum were so heavenly few!

Because 8 x 9 is 72

Life wasn't so easy for poor Katie's mum!

Because 9 x 9 is 81

Mum woke up early to treat herself to some fine tea.

Because 10 x 9 is 90

Poor mum could only rest when it was fine teatime!

Because 11 x 9 is 99

Every morning at school Katie blundered in late.

Because 12 x 9 is 108

Ten Times Table

The ten times table with Katie and Misty at the farm

Katie went looking for rabbits
but instead found a hen.

Because 1 x 10 is 10

When she found all the rabbits she
saw there were plenty.

Because 2 x 10 is 20

The grass on the farm was muddy and dirty.

Because 3 x 10 is 30

Katie thought it would be fun
to be naughty.

Because 4 x 10 is 40

So she snuck up behind her sister,
quietly and swiftly!

Because 5 x 10 is 50

Then wiped the mud from her shoe
onto poor Misty.

Because 6 x 10 is 60

The sound of the lovebirds was heavenly!

Because 7 x 10 is 70

This was a magical day for Misty and Katie.

Because 8 x 10 is 80

The power of the tractor was
amazingly mighty!

Because 9 x 10 is 90

The girls looked tired, "it will soon be
time for bed" mum said.

Because 10 x 10 is 100

The girls began to yawn, so
"time for bed" mum said again!

Because 11 x 10 is 110

"We will come back another day"
mum said gently.

Because 12 x 10 is 120

Eleven Times Table

MILKSHAKE
HEAVEN

The eleven times table with Katie and Misty at Milkshakey Heaven

Misty got a bendy straw from a café called Milkshakey Heaven.

Because 1 x 11 is 11

Katie also had a milkshake straw which was bendy too.

Because 2 x 11 is 22

Suddenly mum heard Misty cry out "Katie's squirting me."

Because 3 x 11 is 33

Mum was cross and asked Katie what she was being naughty for!

Because 4 x 11 is 44

Katie just shrugged and grinned, then with a nifty dive.

Because 5 x 11 is 55

She pulls out the chair just before Misty sits.

Because 6 x 11 is 66

Then poor Misty fell on the floor
of Milkshakey Heaven!

Because 7 x 11 is 77

A scolding from her mother was Katie's fate!

Because 8 x 11 is 88

That ended the trip to the café that sold
milkshakes, so mighty fine!

Because 9 x 11 is 99

''We are leaving NOW!'' mum said again!

Because 10 x 11 is 110

So Misty handed in her empty blue cup
with mum's red empty one.

Because 11 x 11 is 121

Then Katie handed in her cup saying "here's
my one" and "it's dirty too!"

Because 12 x 11 is 132

Twelve Times Table

The twelve times table with Katie and Misty turning things around

Katie and Misty were asking themselves.

Because 1 x 12 is 12

How they could turn their little bit of pocket money into plenty more.

Because 2 x 12 is 24

They both desperately wanted to buy "Mighty Water Squirty Sticks!"

Because 3 x 12 is 36

So mum said "if you carry on being good Misty and don't be naughty Kate."

Because 4 x 12 is 48

Then she would give pocket money to Katie and Misty.

Because 5 x 12 is 60

The girls said "great idea" which mum thought would be heavenly too!

Because 6 x 12 is 72

So Katie tidied Misty's shelf while Misty cleaned Katie's floor!

Because 7 x 12 is 84

The girls worked hard to be able to buy their "Mighty Sticks!"

Because 8 x 12 is 96

Katie even cleaned mum's sunbed and gate.

Because 9 x 12 is 108

But did mum give them pocket money? Yes mum gave them plenty!

Because 10 x 12 is 120

So the girls happily sprayed each other. Then with a smile mum said "and squirt me too!"

Because 11 x 12 is 132

Katie was no longer naughty as being good was much more fun than she'd thought before!

Because 12 x 12 is 144